vjjnf   ᴸ
921 TU   S0-BAD-898

Susienka, Kristen, author
Harriet Tubman
33410016619860   06/17/20

DISCARD
PORTER COUNTY
SYSTEM

Valparaiso Public Library
103 Jefferson Street
Valparaiso, IN 46383

AFRICAN AMERICAN LEADERS OF COURAGE

HARRIET TUBMAN

KRISTEN SUSIENKA

PowerKiDS press™

New York

Published in 2020 by The Rosen Publishing Group, Inc.
29 East 21st Street, New York, NY 10010

Copyright © 2020 by The Rosen Publishing Group, Inc.

All rights reserved. No part of this book may be reproduced in any form without permission in writing from the publisher, except by a reviewer.

First Edition

Editor: Kristen Susienka
Book Design: Michael Flynn

Photo Credits: Cover, p. 1 Print Collector/Hulton Archive/Getty Images; series background Kharchenko Ruslan/Shutterstock.com; p. 5 Donaldson Collection/Michael Ochs Archives/Getty Images; p. 7 Bettmann/Getty Images; p. 9 Universal History Archive/Universal Images Group/Getty Images; pp. 11, 19 Zack Frank/Shutterstock.com; p. 13 (map) pingebat/Shutterstock.com; p. 13 (paper texture) Color Symphony/Shutterstock.com; p. 13 (Underground Railroad) Everett Historical/Shutterstock.com; p. 15 National Geographic Image Collection/Alamy; p. 17 MPI/Archive Photos/Getty Images; p. 21 courtesy of Library of Congress.

Library of Congress Cataloging-in-Publication Data

Names: Susienka, Kristen, author.
Title: Harriet Tubman / Kristen Susienka.
Description: New York : PowerKids Press, [2020] | Series: African American
  leaders of courage | Includes index.
Identifiers: LCCN 2019010494| ISBN 9781725308381 (pbk.) | ISBN 9781725308404
  (library bound) | ISBN 9781725308398 (6 pack)
Subjects: LCSH: Tubman, Harriet, 1822-1913–Juvenile literature. |
  Slaves–United States–Biography–Juvenile literature. | African American
  women–Biography–Juvenile literature. | African
  Americans–Biography–Juvenile literature. | Underground
  Railroad–Juvenile literature.
Classification: LCC E444.T82 S87 2020 | DDC 326/.8092 [B] –dc23
LC record available at https://lccn.loc.gov/2019010494

Manufactured in the United States of America

CPSIA Compliance Information: Batch #CWPK20. For Further Information contact Rosen Publishing, New York, New York at 1-800-237-9932.

CONTENTS

A Special Woman

Harriet Tubman was an important woman in U.S. history. She was born around 1820 in Maryland. She was a **slave**, but she later escaped to **freedom** in the North. She helped many other people escape to freedom too.

Growing Up a Slave

Harriet lived on a **plantation**. When she was about six, she started to work in her owner's house. She was a **servant**. When she was older, she worked in her owner's fields. She picked cotton and other crops.

7

An Injury That Changed Her

When Harriet was 12, she tried to help another slave. Her master wanted to hurt the slave, but Harriet stood in the way. A weight hit her on the head. After that, she sometimes had head pains or fell asleep at strange times.

A Woman with Many Names

Harriet had many names. She was born Araminta Ross. Later, she changed her first name to Harriet. That was her mom's name. When she got married, she took her husband's last name. Later, people called her "Moses."

CAYUGA COUNTY

HARRIET TUBMAN

MOSES OF HER PEOPLE

SERVED UNDERGROUND RAILROAD
FREQUENTED THIS SITE
AFTER THE CIVIL WAR

11

Marriage and Freedom

In 1844, Harriet married John Tubman. He was a free black man. Slaves weren't supposed to get married. That didn't stop Harriet. Within a few years, though, she heard she was going to be sold. In 1849, she escaped to Pennsylvania.

UNITED STATES OF AMERICA

Pennsylvania

All Aboard!

Now, Harriet was free, but she wanted to help other slaves. She joined the Underground Railroad. This was a system that helped slaves make the long, dangerous trip from the South to the North and freedom. Harriet was a conductor, or leader.

During the Civil War

During the 1860s, the United States and 11 Southern states fought each other in the Civil War. Harriet Tubman helped the **Union**. She worked as a nurse, a cook, and a **spy**. She spied on soldiers in the South.

17

After the War

After the war, Harriet Tubman lived in Auburn, New York. She took care of her parents. She worked with another woman to write her **autobiography**. She helped newly freed former slaves and others and fought for women's rights.

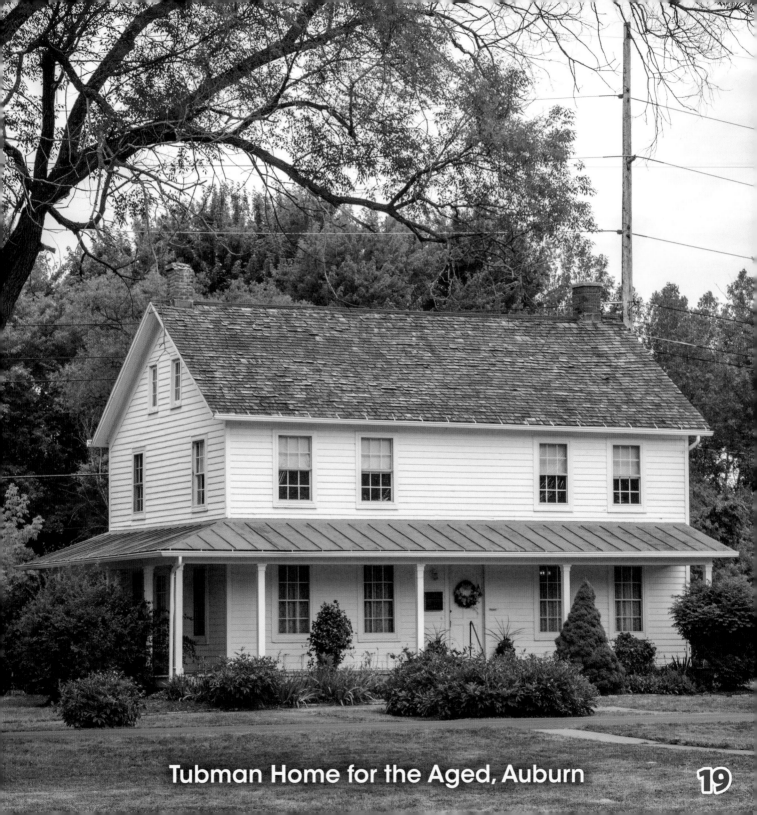

Tubman Home for the Aged, Auburn

19

A Long Life

Harriet Tubman died in 1913. She lived a long life in which she helped others find freedom and happiness. She also helped end slavery forever. She was an important role model for others. Today, people still honor her for her bravery and hard work.

21

THE LIFE OF HARRIET TUBMAN

1820 Harriet Tubman is born.

1832 Harriet suffers a head injury.

1844 Harriet marries John Tubman.

1849 Harriet escapes to freedom and helps other slaves on the Underground Railroad.

1861–1865 Harriet helps the Union during the Civil War.

1913 Harriet dies.

GLOSSARY

autobiography: A book that tells the story of a person's life that is written by the person it is about.

freedom: The state of being free.

plantation: A large farm.

servant: Someone who does jobs such as cooking and cleaning for someone else.

slave: A person "owned" by another person and forced to work without pay.

spy: A person who secretly tries to get information about a country or group for another country or group; also, to try to get this information.

Union: The side of the Northern states in the American Civil War.

INDEX

WEBSITES

Due to the changing nature of Internet links, PowerKids Press has developed an online list of websites related to the subject of this book. This site is updated regularly. Please use this link to access the list: www.powerkidslinks.com/AALC/tubman